Samanta's Story:
One Story, Many Victims

Samanta's Story: One Story, Many Victims

MAIN AUTHOR
DR OLALEKAN OGUNGBEMI

CO-AUTHORS
DR ALI KARIM
HANNAH KIRSCH

StoryTerrace

Text Craig Melvin, on behalf of StoryTerrace
and Olalekan Ogungbemi, Ali Karem and Hannah Kirsch
Design StoryTerrace
Copyright © Olalekan Ogunbemi

First print March 2022

StoryTerrace

www.StoryTerrace.com

CONTENTS

ACKNOWLEDGMENTS

This book was developed based on the coming together of brilliant minds who are determined to put a stop to the menace of women and children trafficking that has plagued Nigeria and the African continent. It will be wrong not to acknowledge the input of my co-authors; the highly esteemed Dr Ali Karim and Hannah Kirsch. Their first-hand experience of dealing with people who have been trafficked provided a solid foundation on which this book was built. It was great meeting with them, sharing ideas and constructive criticism to make this novel authentic yet enjoyable to the reader.

Dr Fatima Dambatta, provided the content of some chapters of the book as well as its proofreading. She was exceptionally helpful in developing the characters.

Miss Opeyemi Akanbi was the legal luminary who enlightened us about legal issues that were portrayed in the book.

My parents, Dr and Mrs. Ogayemi, your feedback, suggestions and motivation were particularly important without which this novel might have been an unfinished manuscript.

To Dr Toyin Aderiye and her lovely husband, Dr Damola

Aderiye, Dr Bunmi Ogayemi and Dr Dimeji Ogayemi, thank you for the support, enthusiasm as well as the days and nights spent proofreading and editing this manuscript.

I further extend my gratitude to Dr Elizabeth Barr and the entire staff of Moray coast medical Practice. All of your support and encouragement was essential during the periods of writer's block.

Special appreciation must go to the John Hopkins community, in particular, Dr Paul Spiegel, Professor at John Hopkins School of Public Health. An outstanding individual who has dedicated his life to training the next generation of highly skilled humanitarian experts.

Finally, I would like to acknowledge with gratitude, the readers of this book. The urge to educate as well as seek your cooperation in putting a stop to trafficking and the exploitation of the vulnerable was the strongest driving force that ensured the completion of this book.

1

MY BIRTHPLACE

Dear Reader,

My name is Samanta Orobosa Matama. I am uniquely myself, but I am also an ordinary person, somebody not unlike your daughter, aunty, sister, niece or mother. Last of all, and importantly for this story, I am a Nigerian. Although I exist only on these pages, I represent the multitude of African girls out there who have had their voices silenced and are secretly crying for help. I hear them, and I speak for them.

I am telling you a complex story of pain, anger, neglect, shame, deceit, crime, institutional shortcomings and systematic failures. I am sharing my story with you, whoever you are: a concerned individual, a leader or influencer, a politician, a member of a law enforcement agency, a member of a governmental or non-governmental organisation or perhaps even someone who has become entwined with the kinds of crimes laid out in this story, either as a perpetrator or as a victim. I am speaking to you all.

This is my story.

I was born in Nigeria 24 years ago. For those of you unfamiliar with my homeland, it is a country of over 200 million people located in West Africa. The country remains a significant presence on the world stage for several achievements. We do have much to be proud of, but Nigeria appears too often in the news in relation to its humanitarian problems.

I was always told as a child that I should count myself lucky to be a citizen of this country. Now that I am an adult, I wonder if I am quite so lucky after all. Hear my story, and then judge for yourself.

As I write this to you, I am propped up in bed in Rome. Why am I here? How did I get to this point? I have lived in Rome for most of my hardscrabble adult life. It is a unique city for obvious reasons: culture, religion, tourism. Rome is the third most populous city in the European Union, with almost three million residents. Rome, as many of you will know, though I did not know it at the start of my journey, is located in a beautiful country called Italy.

Italy, the jewel of Southern Europe, welcomes millions of visitors each year. Some of these visitors, who are then often forced to stay against their will, are illegal migrants, herded through unauthorised routes that enter the country via the back door. Others, complicit in the trafficking of these illegal visitors, are legal visitors coming into the country to exploit the migrants.

Need I add the fact that the majority of these illegal migrants are females like myself who have come to work as commercial sex workers? These sex workers are called 'ashawo' in Nigeria and 'lucciole' in Italy.

On the dark underside of that glittering jewel of Southern Europe, Italy remains an international hub for organised prostitution, despite prostitution being prohibited there by law. Every year, thousands of girls like me from Africa and Asia will find themselves being herded across borders, both land and sea, with the 'help' of human smugglers, for the sole purpose of coming to make money by performing sexual acts for people of the opposite sex or of the same sex, people just like you and me but who pay for sex with a sex worker. These acts will be graphically described later in this story for the purpose of accuracy and because the truth needs to be told. It must not be looked away from. Entire nations with massive prostitution problems continue to struggle due to loop holes and failures in the system.

Somehow, the acts, whether taking place indoors or outdoors, are considered 'legal' if done individually. Considered legal? Please consider this question I would like to ask you, dear reader. How can you stop aiding criminals? Over the years, this sort of trade has developed into a multibillion-dollar industry with untouchable and powerful players. This trading of humans is also indirectly a major earner for criminal syndicate in Thailand and Italy, regardless of whether they 'agree' with it or not. In some cases, citizens from other countries travel to those countries for holidays with a sinister motive in mind: to exploit commercial sex workers in those countries.

If you think Italy and Thailand are in this alone, then you are wrong. New destinations are constantly being acquired in Western countries by international agents, gangs and rich criminal syndicates despite their government's best efforts. The term 'triangle of prostitution' has now become commonly used among commercial sex workers and refers to links between Italy, France and Germany as sites for big illegal businesses.

Dehumanisation of girls like me is at its worst in countries with poor law enforcement, such as Thailand and many parts of Asia, where girls are deceived and then told they will work as house helps. These girls, while working as house help, are sometimes raped and told to carry out sexual acts against their wishes in exchange for basic necessities such as food and water. I will tell you more about this later.

In the American subcontinent, the story is the same. Prostitution is legal in some US states, and girls are imported by criminal gangs from poor countries in the northern and southern parts of the continent. The girls are eventually exploited, forced to pay 80 percent of their daily earnings to these human traffickers over many years in return for their 'freedom'. The story goes on and on.

If, by now, you still don't think there is a problem, then think again.

I was only 17 when I was deceived into making this hopeless journey. It was really tough at the beginning and never really got better. I'm telling you my story not to save myself – it is too late for that – but to save all the other 'Samantas' out there who need your help.

I urge all the international organisations to work together and do something about this ugly trend. As for me, read my story and you'll learn what got me to this point. To the point where I HAD to tell my story.

Was it my initiation in Nigeria? Or was it… No, you'll need to read on. All in good time.

Before I continue with my story, I implore you, do not pity me, but stand up for others who need your help. Let's dive into my story now. I hope it triggers something in you to join the fight.

Yours Sincerely
Samanta Orobosa Matama

2

A FAILED SYSTEM

'm a Nigerian, as you know, and Nigeria is a rich, multicultural and religiously diverse country located in West Africa. It is known as the giant of Africa. My country is blessed with good weather, natural resources and cultivable lands.

Nigeria has four major regions: the north, the south-east, the south-west and the south-south. The south is blessed with a rich cultural heritage and considerable ethnic diversity. I am from the southern part of the south, an oil-rich region whose oil, rather than being a blessing, has become the curse of the land. While the federal government has provided some incentives and infrastructural amenities, it does not warrant the environmental degradation and the high poverty level of the people of these community. The cash generated by these activities ends up in the hands of the federal government or in the pockets of criminals and corrupt politicians. To make things even worse, oil spillages by big multinational companies, local people who try to steal refined products and other actors in my region have damaged our lands and killed our fish, thereby ruining our agriculture. The insatiable thirst for oil has killed nature.

In recent times, unemployment, an increased crime rate, unrest in other regions and terrorism have become the other scourges of the day. Successive governments that made promises to tackle such problems have left them worse. Corruption and greed, fuelled by ethnic intolerance in my country, have prevented the federal system from serving the people. As a result, the gap between rich and poor has continued to widen, with an estimated 65 percent of people living in poverty. My family is one of so many that are part of that 65 percent of 'the poor' in Nigeria. By 'the poor', I mean many families whose daily income can be as low as just 1 dollar a day. My country has been described as having the potential for success by many commentators, but it is yet to achieve this. It is a poverty-stricken, unemployment-ridden nation that, in many ways, has now been surpassed by other African countries that once looked up to it as a shining light.

So now you know, if you didn't already, that Nigeria is a rich country with many poor people, and my family is among the poor. My family, the Matama family, lives in a slum in the southern part of the south. It is important to say that most places in this region either look like slums or are slums. There is poor town planning, and things only get done by accident, rather than design. My father was a teacher and my mother a trader. Theirs were relatively secure jobs, but we barely ate three square meals a day. Like other parents, mine struggled on a daily basis. Both of them worked hard to enable us to afford our basic needs, but we could not always meet them. My two brothers were taught early by my father how to graft and make money during the weekends when there was no school. My parents instilled in me the importance of having an education, and despite the poverty and rampant crime we experienced, I attended a community primary and later, secondary school that cost a small fee. I won many prizes and awards in school; it was a place where I truly excelled. Unfortunately, I had to drop out in my final year of secondary school due to the tragedy that befell my family.

One hot afternoon after school, I returned home, and our house was full of my dad's friends. My dad wasn't there. That was odd, and things seemed out of kilter to me. I greeted the visitors and went into the house, only to see my mum crying. I wasn't too little to not know that something had happened to Dad. What was it?

A few days later, I learned that Dad had been arrested by my country's secret police due to the theft of exam fees from the school where he worked. The total amount that he was accused of stealing was 150 dollars. The police didn't ask him if he stole the money. They only told him that he had to name others that were involved. I cried and cried.

I cried because my dad would never steal. He detested lying and stealing and was content with what he had. I cried because I imagined the pain he must have endured while he was beaten to death.

If it took me until now to tell you that my country's policemen sometimes torture people to death, then it is only because there was so much to tell you about injustice before this. This personal tragedy plays out for people like us across Nigeria on a daily basis.

That was the end of 'Papa joy', as he was popularly known. Deaths like his are not uncommon, so we have always had to move on quickly from their occurrence and their repercussions. In fact, the most common options were to be killed by a deadly disease, an armed robber, civil unrest, the police or, lastly – something that you may not personally believe in – voodoo or juju, as we popularly call it in Nigeria.

So, we had to move on, and I had to immediately step into my father's shoes to support Mum. I took my first job as a hairdresser in a hair salon. It was owned by a woman called Lady Bee. She was tall, beautiful and attractive, and she lived a comfortable life. All I knew about Lady Bee was that she was getting richer by the day and that this could not be attributed to her salon business alone. The other thing was that Lady Bee's workers, who were mainly young girls, had a high turnover rate. By 'high turnover rate', I mean that she was always employing young girls who would suddenly vanish. We sometimes heard good stories about these vanished girls.

'Listen now. Some of these girls have left the shores of the country and are now making good money for themselves.'

This was the word on the street, put about by Lady Bee perhaps, because the sad thing was that we never saw these girls again so that they could tell us of their good fortune in person.

I was glad to get that job with Lady Bee. I felt scared at first, but in what seemed like no time at all, I felt as if I fitted in well. I was barely 15 years old when I got the job. That may seem young to you, but I knew very well that children several years younger than me were doing harder and riskier jobs, so I counted myself lucky.

Lady Bee usually paid us on time. This was a good thing and unusual in Nigeria. The not-so-good thing was that the money was inadequate to buy enough food to last my family a month. My total pay was about 20 dollars a month – not much, but better than nothing. What could I do? I was snared in a poverty trap.

One day while I was working on a customer's hair, teasing the braids through my long-tined comb, clicking my teeth with my tongue in approval as I'd heard the other girls do, I saw an elegant-looking car parked in front of the salon. It was an Anaconda, the latest model. An Anaconda is a car estimated to be worth over 8,000 dollars. I didn't need to do much guessing to know who was in the Anaconda. It had to be Madam Gift, a business associate of Lady Bee who was much discussed among the salon girls.

Many 'madams' in Nigeria are not actually madams. The word describes a very rich woman whose source of wealth cannot be traced. Madam Gift was the current talk of our town following her arrival just less than a year earlier. She, within that year, had acquired two high-rise buildings, one of which was rumoured to be a luxury hotel for the rich.

I was still standing there, my comb frozen at the customer's braid, my mouth slightly open, when a woman of average height and with a fair-skinned complexion stepped out of the car. She stepped out of that car as if she was stepping out of a stretch limo at the Oscars. The first thing I clocked was how flamboyantly dressed she was. She was the very essence of elegant sophistication, with a jewel-strewn neck and a body wrapped in a popular, expensive clothing material in Nigeria called lace. I couldn't properly see the phone in her right hand, but the size of it made me think that its price would have been steep. In her left hand, she held a small purse designed in the shape and colour of a kangaroo. If the phone was not expensive, the purse definitely was.

As she walked in like a queen entering her court, everyone stopped for a moment and paid full attention to her. Short of us all curtsying, the greeting couldn't have been more deferential if we'd tried. We were greeting her as if she was the Queen of England.

Madam Gift returned our adoring, deferential gazes with a warm, welcoming smile. We felt momentarily seen, caught in the radiant glare of her magnificent eyes for a fragmentary moment before she moved on. She turned from us as she walked towards Lady Bee's office, and the smile dropped from her face in an instant.

That smile I now recognise as a symbol of pain, greed and desperation. To think of it now, after all that has happened to me, makes me shudder.

One last thing happened before Madam Gift entered Lady Bee's office. She stopped and turned back for a moment, looked me directly in the eyes and winked at me. This signalled something to me, something that made my heart sink to the soles of my cheap shoes. It was her way of telling me that I was next. It was a non-verbal warning one that attackers usually give their prey. The attackers are the madams, and the prey are the innocent girls. Madam Gift was the madam, and I was the prey.

I know now that I should have picked this up as a sign of danger, a warning sign of imminent and very real danger that was coming towards me. I should have hidden or run away, dropped the long-tined comb and run from that hair salon as fast as my cheaply shod feet could carry me. I should have bolted for my freedom, but I didn't.

Instead, the innocent fool that I was, all I was hoping for was that on her way out she would give some money to everyone, as I'd heard she often did.

I waited, my hands on the braid job, my mind and eyes upon the door to Lady Bee's office... I waited and waited for Madam Gift to come out and gift us all with some cash.

She came out after some time and did just that. This was the first piece of bait on Madam Gift's hook. Soon I would be caught, and all she would have to do then would be to reel me in. Madam Gift had me on her hook from birth, really. Compared to male children, female children are more celebrated in some parts of the country. They are seen as good luck, as they can bring in money from prostitution when they are older. The hairdressing job was just the first sleight of hand in a well-rehearsed and well-performed trick.

3

THE TRICK

The next time I saw Madam Gift, she took me to one side – the thrill of it, being picked out by this highly respected woman.

'Listen to me, girl, and listen good. I'm going to tell you about an amazing life in Europe that I have seen with my own two eyes.'

Madam Gift pointed brightly polished nails at her own two eyes, which were shrouded with cigarette smoke, as she'd just taken a deep drag on her European cigarette and exhaled a blue plume of smoke all around her face. I was hanging on to her every word, as Europe was spoken about in such magical terms that the very idea of going there was akin to a magic carpet ride.

'Girl, hear me. I migrated to Europe 2 decades ago. I know I don't look old enough. That is because I lived the good life over there and didn't age as I would have done back here in Nigeria. I got a decent, well-paying job as a seamstress, a wonderful job with wonderful working conditions. The fabric we worked with was beautiful. Everything was beautiful. See this lace clothing? These are rags compared with the dresses we made in Europe. Just you wait until you can handle them yourself with your own hands in Europe.'

'Madam Gift. Thank you for talking with me,' I said, almost trembling with a heady mixture of excitement and fear –excitement at the thought of Europe and fear that Madam Gift may find me boring or weak or unsuitable in some other way for this magical work. 'Tell me more about the opportunities in Europe.'

'Child, I promise you, as I stand before you as your queen, they are plentiful. You don't have to consider seamstress work as your only option. You could even work as a babysitter or a supermarket cashier.'

My eyes must have widened at the mention of babysitting. That's what I did at home for free. Imagine being paid for sitting around on my phone with a kangaroo-shaped bag on the sofa next to me.

'I, Madam Gift, promise to pay for your journey to make things easy for you so that you can go immediately. I also promise to meet you there once you have arrived to make sure you get settled in without any complications. That is why all my girls love me. I pay for them to go to the dreamland – Europe. I make sure that they are settled in when they get there, and I give them the pick of the best jobs, too. I am like your fairy godmother, girl, as well as your queen. Your wish shall be my command.'

I jigged a little on the spot at this amazing information. It seemed that the opportunity was almost too good to be true. I could feel the floor of the hairdresser's through the right sole of my worn-out shoes. Someday soon, in Europe, I would be picking out the perfect pair of shoes in a beautiful shop. I would be like a modern-day Cinderella choosing the perfect slipper for the ball. Madam Gift poked me in the ribs with an outstretched finger.

'I will set everything up for you, including the driver, the train and the plane tickets. There will be food and accommodations along the way and a pick-up on the other side, and any needs that might arise will be met. Girl, you have nothing to worry about. I have done this so many times for others that it is routine and a smooth process. A smooth process, I tell you – seamless, like the dresses you will be making.'

I remember that the very next Sunday, Madam Gift accompanied me to church along with my family. There were many blessings; there was much happiness. I even saw Madam Gift give the priest a cash donation when she talked with him about me. She was promising a better life for me in the house of the Lord, and we were all overjoyed and gathered together in the pew to pray for my success.

What blasphemous lies it all was.

Madam Gift took me aside outside the church and told me to prepare for leaving in about two weeks. My pulse quickened when I heard this news. So quick! There must be an incredible shortage of good workers to make my future employers want me in Europe so quickly. The beam on my face shone from ear to ear. What thrilling things to be thinking about. Two weeks could drag so slowly in my normal life. One week felt much like every other in the hair salon. Now, in 14 days, I would be embarking upon the journey of my lifetime. It was too good to be true. I remember thinking these exact words – 'too good to be true' – especially after the awful murder of my father and the grief my family had been forced to bear. Now I would be able to provide for all of them, just as my beloved father had done before me. I felt so blessed and proud to be able to do this for my family.

I walked home from the church with my family, and, I have to tell you, it felt as if my feet were three feet off the ground. My mother held my hand tightly and told me how proud she was of me. I felt my heart almost burst with pride at her saying this. It was the most pitch-perfect moment I had ever had. I was excited. I was expectant. And I celebrated. Madam Gift had told me before she got back into her eight-thousand-dollar car that she had to return to Europe but that she would contact my family when she had a more specific time set up and more information about who would be picking me up

My friends at the salon warned me that this offer sounded too good to be true. They'd heard rumours that some of the people who headed to Europe never arrived or were sent back. Some rumours came from the hair-sweeping women that the girls who reached Europe struggled to make a good life. Only a few families had ever had the good fortune to then follow their girls to Europe. For every single success story, there were dozens of failures, they said.

I swept these thoughts away with a cluck and a smile to myself in the mirror. These girls were just jealous. The sweeps and cleaners at the salon were at the lowest rung on the beauty ladder. *They would never be offered such prestigious work in Europe*, I thought. My desire to be right and for everything to work out like a fairy tale blinded me to their warnings.

My family, whom I loved very much, struggled with food shortages, poor daily earnings, a lack of job opportunities and a fear of petty crime and government corruption resulting in the abuse of innocent citizens – the abuse (and murder) of innocent citizens such as my father. Holding these truths up to the salon mirror rather than listening to the muttering of the cleaners, I decided that, in spite of what people might be saying, I *had* to take Madam Gift up on this offer.

I waited for the call to come through for two weeks. When I wasn't working at the salon, I would sit by the bench upon which my mother had placed the family pay-as-you-go mobile phone, the only place near our shack that got a signal, a weak signal but a signal, nevertheless. After two weeks and five days, I was beginning to think it had all been a dream, that it would never happen and that I would be working for a pittance in the salon for the rest of my life. Europe was a mirage that was disappearing fast. Then, out of the blue, after three weeks and one day, Madam Gift called my mother's number. My mother took the call and held her free hand to her head in happiness and relief.

'Samanta. Daughter. Everything has been set. A man will come to our home in the morning to pick you up by 5 a.m. Madam Gift, God bless her, said that you should be ready to go immediately for a long but easy journey.'

My mother hugged me for the longest time.

4

THE INITIATION

They picked me up, and then we drove for what felt like a long, long time into the night. It was still very dark when they turfed us off the bus. I was scared – normal scared compared to the scared that came later, but scared all the same. I was 17 years of age and being herded like cattle on the way to the slaughterhouse.

We were a total of 11 girls in this shipment. It was dark, and we could not see where we were going, but we kept going. The grasses were tall, and I could hear chirping sounds and the sounds of the night wind. All I could see in the dark were the whites of the eyes of my 10 fellow victims, for victims is what we were. We just didn't know it yet.

We walked and walked, and then we slowed down. I thought we were at our destination, but it was just a bridge to cross. After walking for close to three hours, we finally arrived. The scene was like one from a horror movie. There was a small hut set in the middle of a clearing surrounded with several hurricane lamps that lit it up. My eyes squinted at the bright light we had been prodded into. Until then, we had been forced to stumble along in the darkness. I think I preferred the darkness to what I was confronted with in that circle of evil light.

As we approached the door of the hut, forced forwards by those I soon came to think of as our captors, an elderly man most likely in his late 60s came out and laughed at the sight of us all. It was a crazed laugh, one that made me tremble with fear. I needed to use the toilet urgently but was too scared to ask. The scene before me was terrifying. The clearing was littered with skulls and bones that looked like human remains. In our local dialect, the old man told Madam Gift something that I didn't hear. It is awful, being talked about when you don't know what your aggressor is saying. Madam Gift nodded at the man and turned to the 11 of us.

'Take off your clothes and underwear,' she commanded.

That was the first thing she had said to me since wishing me goodbye and God bless on the steps of the church. A few minutes later, amid half-muffled sobs, we were all stark naked in the cold of the night. I was beginning to shiver slowly. Cold and fear are a potent mix.

The man started intoning voodoo songs and muttering incantations. He then went into the hut and brought out a small clay pot. He poured a liquid that I think was alcohol into it and started dancing towards us. The 11 of us had been formed into a horseshoe shape by our handlers. The first girl at the bottom of the horseshoe, the unlucky one, was Carol, or Caro as we said the name in Nigeria. As the juju man danced towards her, you could see the fear in her face. Caro was trying to suppress a scream and was struggling with her fight-or-flight natural reaction, as we all were. It was just that he had gone to her first. It was almost as bad watching, knowing that you would be the one to have his attention soon, as it was to be the one he was facing. The juju man bent down at eye level with Caro's genitals and used a small sharp blade to cut off some of her pubic hair. He held this stolen lock of her pubic hair, pinched between his forefinger and thumb, before sprinkling a couple of the hairs into the clay pot as one would sprinkle seasoning into a stew. The juju man then moved in a jerky motion behind Caro and raised his hand and his blade to the back of her neck.

The 10 of us, waiting our turn, collectively gasped. Caro stood stock-still, tears pooling and dropping silently from her wide eyes, and waited. The juju man made a swift, deep cut, and blood poured out of the back of Caro's neck. He took the remaining hairs pinched in his fingers and mixed them with the blood, then came around to the front of her. To Caro's face, the juju man wailed in a horrible, high-pitched, keening voice that she was to swear by the mixture that if she rebelled or reported her mistresses, she would die suddenly.

'DIE SUDDENLY.'

The juju man swept his outstretched arm around the circle of rancid yellow light. Our eyes followed, taking in, once more, the human skulls and bones.

One by one, each of us endured this initiation ritual, a putrid process that we all had to pass through, with the talisman using the same blade on each of us with limited sterilisation. My legs were like jelly. I believed that I was going to pass out when he cut the back of my neck.

I hoped against hope that this was the end of the ritual, a ghastly rite of passage that we could forget and move on from. My country has a dark past when it comes to voodoo. Voodoo is used as a tool of fear and control and is highly effective. We 11 girls were terrified of the whole process and what it meant for our future safety.

At the edge of the light was a row of shallow graves into which we were laid in groups of four while incantations went on overhead. At the time, I felt that the bottom of that grave was the worst place I would ever be in my entire life. In the years since that night, there have been countless cars, street corners, even slightly comfortable beds that have been far worse places to lie in.

Further foul rituals were performed upon us as a covenant to keep us from telling anyone about everything we had encountered that night or would encounter from this day forwards. This was on pain of death. These individuals were deadly serious, and I totally believed them.

By the time I was dropped back outside my family shack in the morning, I was bone tired. I slept countless hours, and when I awoke, my family was gathered around me. I thought for one moment that I was, perhaps, on my deathbed. No, I had been through that the night before, and now I was safe at home with my loved ones. They asked what had happened to me with Madam Gift and her people, and I lied to them like a pro to protect them. I told them that we'd had an overnight orientation, and I was most likely going to be posted as a sales manager in one of the big cities.

Everyone at home was so excited for me, dancing around and whooping. I was silent because I knew this was a lie, and the truth was slowly dawning on me about my dangerous choice. The days from that moment seemed to both fly by and drag in the most unbearable way. With each day that passed, I became more mysterious to myself – more withdrawn, more unhappy. Anyone who'd been a sceptic and taken a close look would have seen the sadness written all over my face. It was sadness etched with fear. If that nightmare experience had been a taste of what was to come, I wished that I could join my father in the afterlife at that moment rather than face the unspecified horrors that awaited me.

Two weeks after our initiation, word reached my home that everything was set for us to go to Europe. I knew that

I had to go for the sake of making money for my family, but my feet became heavy, and I was unsure if I really wanted to make the journey. But it appeared to me that the deal was done and that there was no going back. I was given an address to come in to sign my contract. When I got there, I saw everyone smiling and well dressed. The other girls and I were treated with dignity, given food and expensive drinks. It was as if the voodoo initiation ceremony hadn't happened. It was surreal and destabilising. I was already beginning to think that I was losing my mind slightly. Could these same well-dressed, hospitable people be the ones that had marched us through the night to a wicked voodoo ceremony, cut us, drained our blood and simulated burying us alive?

I had never had a man look at my private area before that night. I was 17 and a virgin. The first one to do so was that juju man with his mad stare and sharp knife. I will never forget that, even after all the injustices and degrading acts I have been forced through in the years since.

After the short ceremony, the polar opposite of the hurricane lamp–lit horrors, we were given papers to sign. The documents were opened to the last page, which said, 'Now you have read all the terms and conditions. If you are happy with these, sign below.'

I had not read any terms and conditions, and I did not have any idea what the job was about. I asked the man who was in front of me holding my letter.

'Excuse me, sir. Would it be possible to read the contents of the letter?'

The man looked straight into my eyes after the question and smiled icily, as if to say, *What is wrong with you?*

'Please sign and let me leave.'

This was the fifth time in the space of a month that I was seeing that smile, that dead-eyed smile that denoted pain and shame. The man shook his head, his meaning made very clear, the meaning being to tell me it was not possible. I shook from tip to toe, fully dressed in my finest clothes yet feeling as naked before him as I had when stripped in front of the juju man on that freezing, terrifying night. This moment, and what it would be leading to, was more terrifying than anything the juju man could cook up.

I picked up the pen, not knowing what else to do other than sign the letter. After I signed, he smiled the dead-eyed smile with a hint of self-satisfaction and muttered, 'Well done.' He then walked away very quickly, handing the document to Madam Gift to cross- check that we had all signed. Afterwards, music was played, and more food was brought in for us as a celebration, but it was not the girls celebrating – it was our slave masters. They had just hit a jackpot, and we, unluckily, had just been sold into slavery.

5

THE JOURNEY

The journey began early in the morning at around 5 a.m., as had been originally stated, when a driver sent by Gift arrived at my home to take me to the train station. I'd already been informed that a passport would be organised for me, as well as train and plane tickets and all accommodations. It had the makings of a rather pleasant holiday. Had I not already experienced the voodoo ritual and the forced contract signing, perhaps I would have been excited or, at least, expectantly nervous. All I had to do was pack what I needed and be ready to go.

I tried to steady my shaking hand as I packed the humble things that I owned into a small, cheap suitcase that a friend at the salon had given me as a going away present. I may as well have travelled in the clothes I was standing in because I'd soon discover these clothes would be of no use to me. It would all be replaced with cheap, thin nightclub attire soon enough. When I wasn't forced into wearing that, I was just sleeping and didn't care what I was wearing anyway.

At the time, I thought that the night before I left was a terrible night's sleep. Little did I know that it would be the safest night of sleep I would ever have again. I was at home, safe and loved. I wasn't yet enslaved to a wicked system, though technically, because I had signed the contract, I was. The only thing that was protecting me from my fate was time. Time can be spent, but it can't be bought. I had lain on my childhood bed, staring at the ceiling and occasionally checking the clock. The weary arms wound around to 4.30 a.m., and I hit the alarm in the split second before it clicked on mechanically and made the high-pitched, trilling beep. The alarm was right to be high-pitched and shrill. It was a warning alarm for the days and years ahead. I should have taken heed and fled out into the fields before dawn. What would have become of my family if I had? Would my little sister Joy have been taken in my place? I'll never know because I was already chained to the injustice of it all. From the voodoo viciousness onwards, I was ensnared by the system. Many before me had been snapped in the same trap, and many after would follow.

I said goodbye to my siblings and mother, crying from sorrow but trying to pass it off as happiness.

'These are happy tears,' I said, unsure about how much my family believed me. I had taken a sacred vow that I believed, if broken, would kill my family. I was under pain of their deaths, and there was no way that I was going to do that to them. I felt that I had got myself into this mess and

I had to go through with it. I was 17.

I did not know when I would ever see my family again, but I did know that they were proud I was going so that they could all have a better life. There was still a hopeful part of me that believed I would be getting them a better life. Whatever it was I would be doing in Europe, my most fervent hope was that it would ease their suffering. I thought of my father, what he would have done in my situation, and I tried to be as strong as him. I thought about his death and the bravery it would have taken to endure what he'd endured. It made the tears flow all the more freely. I turned at the door to our shack and vowed to bring my loved ones with me to Europe one day soon.

The man who was picking me up said his name was Goodluck. This was a bad omen; it wasn't bringing me any good luck – that was for sure. Goodluck told me that he had been taking girls for this first part of their journey for a while. That was pretty much all he said. He didn't speak much after that, instead opting to turn on the radio to the local news. I stared out the window, dreaming of what was to come. I kept flip-flopping between hope and despair. I was excited to be learning a new language and hoped it would not be too difficult to pick up. I had been good in school, quick to learn, before I had had to leave and go out to earn money in the hair salon for my family. I also hoped that I would learn the ways of the new country as fast as possible. Have you ever had that feeling when you are travelling somewhere new and you try to imagine what it will be like based on what you have read, heard or seen of it? I was in a place of underlying dread but with the mild expectation that going to this new, magical, faraway place may be a good life experience in some ways. I hoped that, once I made it to Europe, the people would be kind, not like the Nigerian people I had met so far since I agreed to take the offer that Madam Gift was extending to me.

I gazed out at the rising dawn. The trip to the train station seemed to be taking a long time, but I was probably just tired. My head nodded from time to time, and then I would snap back awake. It was the start of a lifetime of fearful, fitful sleep that had me longing for death due to the fear and deprivation life was plunging me into and out of.

The car finally came to a stop, and Goodluck got out, telling me to stay put. The dawn was now fully upon us, and I could see him meeting with another man standing next to a big white van. This place didn't seem like the train station to me. There were no buildings and no other people with packed bags, just a parking lot with the two men talking to one another and looking back at me occasionally. The fear rose up my spine, past the scab where the juju man's knife cut was slowly healing and settled on the crown of my head. Despite the cool air of the morning, beads of sweat formed on my brow.

Goodluck came back and asked me to get my stuff and follow him. I complied, for what else could I do? He could have killed me with one blow of his hand. We walked up to the other man, who didn't say a word. He looked me up and down and got into the driver's seat of the van. The door slid open, and Goodluck told me to get in for the rest of the journey. I followed his command, even though something felt off. Very off. I felt about as human as the suitcase at my side.

In the dim light inside the van, I could make out the sight of many other girls, some younger, some older than me. All of them had packed bags next to them. Some of them were talkative and excited; others seemed quieter and more pensive about the situation. I sat back and went back into my thoughts of Europe. I wanted to keep myself to myself. There was a dread of what had happened with the juju man that kept creeping up inside me. That was the last time I had been gathered with a group of girls like this.

We drove all day until darkness, stopping only at a few checkpoints but never for food. Finally, we arrived at another parking lot. This time, all of us girls were asked by the men up front to exit the van. We stood there in the darkness until another group of men arrived. A private discussion happened; then the new group came to look us up and down as if we were cattle. They named prices, and one by one, we women were singled out and separated until none were left. I was given a price on my head as well and then led towards a new van. I stopped stock-still for a moment because I thought that I'd heard Gift's voice on the phone with one of the men. I could not be sure. Perhaps I was imagining things. It had been a long day. I didn't stay stock-still for long. I was shoved from behind by the man on the phone and propelled into my new mode of transport.

This cycle of one stop after another continued over the next few days. Slowly, it dawned on me that there may be no train after all. I was still in magical thinking mode – so hopeful. Maybe it was just cancelled, so they decided to go by car instead. My mind sluggishly churned over the facts. How would I get to Europe, though? I realised that I hadn't yet seen my passport. I haven't seen my passport to this day.

While in the beginning the men were speaking a local Nigerian dialect, as time and the miles passed, tongues turned, and the men were then speaking a different language. Arabic maybe? The terrain was turning, too. It was no longer very fertile or green. The weather seemed to be humid, and every time they took me out of the van for those infrequent stops, there was lots of sand everywhere.

We finally arrived at a nondescript building, and they took us all inside. I was put in a room with other women and told to wait. The women all looked hungry and tired, even more hungry and tired than I was. It looked as if they had been there for days. Maybe they had. I didn't know what to think or how to feel. This wasn't the journey I'd expected. *Maybe my expectations were too high*, I kept telling myself. Maybe this was the hard path necessary to get there.

It is Europe, after all. Maybe the utopia of Europe had to be hard-won.

It felt as if I had remained in that room forever. It may even have been a week or two. The men there spoke more of a foreign language than a Nigerian one. *It has to be another country*, I was thinking. Could it be Niger? What's north of Niger? Morocco? Algeria? Libya? I knew we must've been in one of those. So, we were at least closer to Europe.

We were barely fed over that week or two. I got one meal a day, two if I was lucky. The meals never consisted of very much – a small piece of bread, some rice, a tiny piece of meat every now and then. It wasn't like the fufu and cassava back home. It was some kind of strange food, alien to me.

The men were rude and stern. They yelled at us women to keep it down when we cried in hunger or fatigue. They denied us blankets, pillows and mattresses. Sometimes they took a woman away alone, not to be seen again. If the woman was seen again, she came back with bruises and silence, never once discussing what had happened. There were rumours that the women were being abused by the men.

Raped.

I had been lucky up to that point not to be isolated. My back was starting to hurt from sleeping on the hard dirty ground and from days of sleeping in the back of a van. The wound on the back of my neck had somehow got infected and was hot and tender to the touch. I told myself that it was OK, that my young body could handle it. It was better that

I went through this instead of my mother or siblings. I was made to do this, so I told myself, for my family, for Europe.

Finally, after many more days, the men came and escorted us women out, grabbing us by our arms forcefully and pushing us ahead towards another group of vans. After the eternal darkness of the room, the light of the sun burned my eyes. The van took off at speed, but we weren't in it for long before arriving at the waterfront. We were pushed and prodded onto a makeshift small boat. My mind was racing. This couldn't possibly be how we would be heading to Europe. What about the aeroplane and the passport? I knew then that something was really off. It stank more than the water lapping under the boat. I kept telling myself that it was all OK because the journey was still happening. It was the destination that mattered.

We were on that boat for days and weeks, with barely any food or water, in a small room below the deck. Many of the other girls were seasick. Not me. I always had a strong stomach. We waited down there for word of our arrival, but that day never seemed to come. I was terrified that the boat might not make it, that it might capsize in a storm. The other women told stories of people drowning at sea on this journey. 'What if another boat found us?' we muttered. Were we even allowed to arrive by boat? Word was that some women had already crossed and been sent back. I was scared at all this, but I tried not to show it. Nothing else mattered. I was almost there.

When I finally saw land from the boat, my eyes pooled with an ocean of tears. My heart was pounding with excitement. I could feel and hear it over the throb of the boat's engine. The journey was strewn with pain and obstacles, but I'd made it! The better life I was promised and the better life I'd be able to give my family back home were within arm's reach at the bottom of the slippery gangplank.

6

THE BETRAYAL

landed in Italy. Somehow I survived and I made it. The horrors of my journey so far had drained me, but as I alighted from that small foul-smelling boat, dragging my battered suitcase behind me, I felt a flicker of hope that just maybe it would all be worth it.

It was definitely not the arrival I had imagined. Back in Nigeria, my naive mind had conjured up a star-like arrival at the airport, with me dressed in a beautiful outfit, with paparazzi and flair and possibly surrounded by Italian actors just like I had seen in the movies we watched back home. Instead, I dragged my body, reeking with stench from bodily fluids that were not all mine, to an unmarked van waiting to take my sea mates and me to a migrant detention centre. This, at sea-level, was my lowest ebb, everything I had hoped for washed up on this litter-strewn beach.

Arrivals by sea from Libya are common. Over 100,000 people a year cross this migrant route hoping to make a better life for themselves. The vessels are unseaworthy and overstuffed, as ours was. They are fuelled with the bare minimum of fuel and then abandoned, with all the passengers on board, if they don't make it. They certainly have more fuel than water, which is provided on a survival ration basis. Thousands of migrants don't make it. They end their lives in a watery grave, unmarked, unnoticed.

I'll tell you what it feels like to arrive at a detention centre. It feels at once both frightening and also like a bit of a relief. I mistakenly thought that perhaps my ordeal had come to an end, that I would receive better treatment from the Italians here, that, once this horrendous process of being checked in at the detention centre was over and we were allowed into the country, I would finally have some dignity and would be able to begin the work I had gone through all of this for.

The woman who came to the detention centre to claim me had me sign a contract saying that I would work for her for two years. My documents were given to this woman, and I was released into her care. It is with care that I say 'care'. It wasn't exactly care but rather a long way from it. Also, looking back, I see that the arrangement between the woman and the detention centre must have been corrupt in some way or another.

However, on that day I breathed a huge sigh of relief once she took me to her house and explained that I would begin work the next day. She showed me to a room that she said I would be sharing with two other girls who would 'work' with me. Then she gave me some clothes to change into and asked me to come out once I was done showering. I came out to the sight of a delicious spread on the table, and I cried as I had my first proper meal since this ordeal had begun.

Madam was very sweet that first night, asking me questions about my family back in Nigeria, and naively I told her everything – about my father's death and how hard things were for my family, about how I had to leave school and work in the salon before Madam Gift found me. It is only now I realize that this was also a tactic. They wanted to confirm that the girls they brought did not have anyone powerful enough to come looking for them, the rejects of the society.

She asked me to go to bed early as I would be having an early morning orientation the next day. I knelt down at her feet and took her hands into my hands. I thanked her with reverence – my guardian angel had come at last. I promised her that I would be the hardest worker she had come across.

By my estimate it was somewhere around midnight when it happened. The little sleep I had before it happened was my first dreamless one in months. I did not hear when he came in, but when he tapped me and his face came into focus, somehow my scream, a mixture of confusion and fear, got caught in my throat. I can still taste the white-hot blinding pain as he thrust into me, still fresh despite all the pain that has come after it.

The next morning Madam gave me a once-over, and with

a sneer at the corner of her lips, she asked if I had enjoyed my orientation – after all, I had said I was eager to begin 'work'. My cries and protests that this was not the work I had signed up for and that I would do literally anything else fell on deaf ears. She calmly reminded me that I had signed a contract and that, if I knew what was good for me, I would go and get ready, as I had a lot of work lined up that day. Gone was the mother like figure of the previous day – she had been replaced by a brisk businesswoman.

She showed me the contract that I had signed and told me that there was nowhere I could go. The madam helped me apply for asylum as a means to control me for years as I waited for the decision to be processed.

A prickle of realisation travelled through my body. Without my documents and without money, plus the debt, I was enslaved and had no choice other than to work for the madam.

I was alone.

I thought about my family, my choices, the initiation ceremony and the oath we had been made to swear and how the idea of Europe had been a fantasy that I should have known was not going to be a reality. I thought back to the day I had first clapped eyes on Madam Gift. I should have lowered them and carried on combing those braids.

I thought about how much I had had to go through to get to Europe. Then I thought about how it would only be getting harder from that point onwards, without a means to get out. I hadn't even begun the work that I had been duped into coming here to do.

I kicked myself for not having asked what Europe would be like. I was young. My family wanted the best for me and for the rest of the family, and I just hoped it would be a chance for a better life. I think I realised at that point just what a tough operator Madam Gift must have been to rise through all of this to get to the point that she was the most senior woman in the operation. I am sure that the men above her terrified her, as she terrified me, but she managed to stay above water all that time and tell so many lies, sell so many dreams. She was a seamstress seductress spinning her sewing machine thread full of lies. I'd been stitched up by her, my arms sewn to my body, the back of the dress wide open for all the men to see. She was the juju of all this, not that voodoo guy in the woods. He was just a two-bit showman. Madam Gift was the truly terrifying ringmaster of the freak show.

As I wailed on the floor of the room that was now occupied by five other sleeping girls, back from their night of work, one of them woke up and told me to shut it or she would shut me up. 'So, you thought there was manna in Italy, hey?' she hissed.

7

THE BIG BUSINESS

How does one describe the day-to-day of doing sex work? It's hard to put into words because, at first, it is so overwhelming that it is almost beyond comprehension or mere words. Then, as the shock of the sheer brutality subsides, a sort of numbness descends. It's the only way to endure.

I'm not going to tell you again about the first time. That is too upsetting to revisit. Let's just say it was the polar opposite of all my hopes for that rite of passage in my life, which was something I had dreamed would be between me and somebody I loved rather than a man who had paid a premium to 'take my cherry'. I hated the act, hated the proximity and hated the intrusion into my body.

Those who have had to endure repeated rape know that I need say no more. It is too traumatic to talk about. Let me just say to the rest of you wishing to understand the nature of sex work, particularly slave trade sex work – think back to any unpleasant but necessary internal examination that you had. Let's throw in dentistry if you like. Now imagine that the person deep inside you hated you and wanted to cause you a lot of pain.

'Do no harm? 'These men did me harm.

Repeatedly.

After some weeks of this repetitive brutality, I would wake up late in the day, exhausted, numb, with bruises on my body, and in my brain, flashes of men on top of me would appear that I would try to shake away.

There was no time to rest. I was constantly berated by the madam to get more clients, constantly reminded of my debt and the power the organisation had over me. I felt constantly threatened, always running on adrenaline. The lack of sleep didn't help. I was awake all night, servicing men. Then, when daylight came, there was no space to sleep properly on the floor in a room full of exhausted women.

There were no days off. Every day was a recurrent nightmare.

I tried to talk to some of the women, but madam had created a hierarchy. There was no way through it. Madam Gift was at the top of this pyramid. Imagine how tough she must have been to get to that point. As much as I hated her and was terrified of her, there was a small part of me that admired her survival instinct. Down the levels of this pyramid were the madams of this brothel, the girls who ran the other girls, the girls who still worked, me (a new girl at the time) and then the dead. The dead were at the bottom of the pyramid because they couldn't speak and had no way to rise to the top. They were literally entombed by this structure. In Italy, where I actually performed the task that the sex slave trade had gone to all the effort to ship me in for, the pyramid made the juju's open graves look like a nice lie-down.

When word reached the madam that I had talked, I was severely reprimanded. Not all the cuts and bruises came from the punters.

One of the girls always collected the money. I was very apprehensive about clients at the beginning and did everything I could to avoid them. Madam beat me for not bringing in enough, and I had to get paid in order to avoid physical retribution. After enough beatings from the madam, the brutal penetration by the men became slightly preferable

So much for my dream of discovering Europe. I was sent out in all kinds of weather to work, come hell or high water, night after night in the rain, shivering in skimpy clothes, waiting for strange men to come and take me. Then, at the turning of the year, being so hot in summer, there was never enough water. I thought I was going to die of thirst. If one of the men didn't kill me first, I thought, then dehydration could be relied upon to do the job. I thought that one of the men would probably kill me in the end, either by their own hands or by something more insidious, something viral, a slow and painful death – but murder, nonetheless.

Madam told me I had to do more men. The other sex workers told me that three to four men a night was common. That's what they did, and I should be able to do that, too. It was a productivity target that I had to hit.

I was utterly distressed, utterly traumatised, utterly horrified.

All the while, I was forced to work long hours with no rest. If I was sick, I still had to work. If I was menstruating, I still had to work. If I became pregnant, I would still have to work. As soon as I'd given birth or had the abortion, I'd be put back to work.

When I got my period and wasn't provided with any sanitary materials, I was still forced to work. I depended on these people totally for my well-being, and they betrayed me. Imagine the ignominy of having no sanitary products and then also having to give a man access to your most private of areas while menstruating. Evil people.

I saw one of the other girls get pregnant. This was a result of her being sold at a premium to a man who didn't want to use a condom. The madam forced her to have an abortion and return to work immediately. I was terrified of getting pregnant. There was nothing I could do to stop a man if he wanted to pay the madam more and not use a condom. It was the ultimate sex slave trap. The thing that was the most perilous for me made the machine more money.

I was regularly beaten by the clients and the madam. Sometimes, when the sex work was very rough, there was little distinction between the two, other than the fact that, with the former, I ran the risk of getting pregnant, being torn or ruptured in an intimate place or suffering any number of other things that would stop me from being able to work and get me beaten until I went back to work again. It made the fretting that I'd done on the journey about that small septic cut on the back of my neck almost laughable.

Talking of laughter, I didn't laugh anymore. I didn't speak much at all. I'd become quiet, a ghost almost, apart from the bare necessities needed to transact with the madam and the men. I gave up talking to the other girls and became part of the wall of silence that I'd come up against when I arrived. Some girls disappeared in the night, and new girls arrived to replace them. I ignored them, as the girls had ignored me when I first arrived. Talk can get you a beating. It may even cost you your life.

There was never any food or water given to us while we were working. Like a stray dog, the best you could do was to sneak a sip of the man's drink or any food left lying around. I hated myself for having to stoop so low and cried at the thought of my mother and sister seeing me in this place, acting this way.

I learned the art of disassociation while I was with clients, trying to go to a mental place where I felt as though I was not inside my body while they were inside me. I became adept at watching myself being violated from above. I learned not to care what happened to 'her' down there.

One of the girls was so distraught that she refused to work and tried to give the madam some money that she'd smuggled for herself. The madam grabbed the iron and burned her. There was no way out. Another time, a man didn't have money to pay me, but he did have a knife, so I gave him what he wanted. Then, of course, I was beaten by the madam for not bringing enough money to her. It was a vicious cycle, a cycle of viciousness. The men didn't have to use condoms if they didn't want to, and it was too dangerous to say no to them; I was beyond scared of the consequences.

Sex with men in their homes: 100 euros.

Sex with men in their cars: 50, 30, 20 euros, depending on what they wanted.

Giving the money over to madam after all that was so very hard. The money was my way home. Girls came back beaten because, when the men couldn't finish, they would begin beating you instead. Those girls that could, fled.

Walking down the road every night, with cars passing by, I experienced fear of them stopping and fear of them not stopping because then how would I pay madam?

Every month I had to give €200 to Jennifer, my madam, as rent for my space in the street and €250 as rent for the house where I slept – in the kitchen, one of the coveted spots. I also gave €50 per week for groceries. For other expenses, such as electricity and gas, she asked me for €300 per month. That was all. All that remained was to repay my debt of €50,000, and I would be free.

8

THE CONSEQUENCES

began to have bouts of uncontrollable and unpredictable crying at night. The hardest aspect of this was trying to be quiet. If I woke the other girls, they would be angry with me and tell the madam. Luckily, I made one friend, Angel, who slept next to me. Angel and I never really spoke; that's not what any of us did. She is one of those people that just has a comforting aura. She is average in height, with features that would not send tongues wagging when she enters a room. However, there is something about Angel that draws you in, something that makes her instantly likeable. Was it because we were of the same nationality or could it have been the fact that she understood what extreme poverty was – being able to go days without having a meal to eat.

She had been in the business for 2 years before I came in and had experienced the same initial problem with adapting to the pitiful life. One night, when I was shuddering with silent sobs, Angel reached out a hand and held mine. We slept hand in hand from that day on. I say 'day' because it was always daylight by the time we got to lie down.

By then, I'd lost my appetite and was barely eating more than one meal a day. I'd lost nearly 10 kilograms, unintentionally, over the course of that first six months in Europe. When I think about how, when I first started at the hair salon, I used to talk with the other girls about our weight, I can barely believe it. I'd lost more than just weight and my appetite. Over those first six months, I'd lost my appetite for life. It's not that I wanted to die; I just didn't want to live. Every day was a living hell, so even the hell promised by the juju man sounded more restful than this. The problem was twofold. One, I didn't want the painful death, slow torture or beheading that would be my lot if I overstepped the line. Two, the juju ceremony made me promise that I would fulfil my pledge or my family would DIE. Beyond superstition, I totally believed now that these people were capable of killing my family. Corruption had killed my father. These people were many times more evil than the people who'd killed my father.

I had to go on.

Activities that were once pleasurable for me, such as painting my nails, putting on new styles of make-up and watching comedy movies on TV became devoid of meaning. The pampering felt like work, just dressing up for the men, and I failed to see the funny side of any light-hearted drama on a screen after a real life like this. I lost interest in everything I had once loved. The idea of being in contact with my mother and sister made me weep in shame. I felt utterly cut off from the life I had left and the person I had once been. It was as if I had entered the body of a new and vastly more unhappy person.

Sleep was still a terrible issue. I had no memory of the last good night of sleep I'd had since leaving Nigeria. I vaguely remembered feeling contented and sleeping well the night Madam Gift promised me a better life, but I was way beyond feeling tired by this point. I just felt numb.

In my daily hell of a life, I felt guilt and shame. That was exhausting, and I had no energy left for other emotions, apart from the thought of what I would say to my mother, so I felt nothing instead. The only constant thought I had was that I was in serious debt and that there was no way out until it was paid off. This debt was an insidious tool. It was a nominal number of outrageous proportions placed upon us to keep us under the yoke of the masters. That we girls fell for this ruse and continue to do so is one of the biggest injustices of this whole racket. The masters somehow convince us that we owe this enormous sum and then set us to work on our backs to pay it off while all the while they take the lion's share of our earnings for themselves. It is a hopeless position to be caught in. When will it ever be paid off?

After my body had been shuddering with silent sobs for hours one night, Angel whispered to me that there was a way I could cheer up because she, too, had felt this crushing depression. I asked Angel how she'd done this. Angel put her lips to my ear and whispered her two lines of magical thinking.

'You know, girl, pretend you are someone else, a secret agent on a mission. That's what I did. You know, like in a movie.'

You know, I felt cheered by this idea and had the best night's sleep since leaving my home – two hours of solid sleep, at least. When I awoke, I resolved to take Angel's advice and pretend to be undercover to convince myself that this was a job I must do for the greater good of a department I was serving in the government. I had a think about which department I was serving and decided that it would be a department for women, even though I'm sure there wasn't one in either Italy or Nigeria. It calmed me to think that I was on a mission for the Women's Department – deep, deep undercover. It gave me a sense of purpose and was a relief from the numbness of the day-to-day. I look back on this period now and am amazed at how long I managed to sustain myself with this make-believe. I also remember that I'd not long since put down my dolls and imaginary tea parties, so it wasn't that big a leap. I like to think that if I'd been able to finish school, I might have taken up a government job at a department like this or even had a career as an actor in which I got to do make-believe for a living.

This personal subterfuge got me through. When I was beaten by a man who didn't want to pay or who simply enjoyed being rough, I convinced myself that I was fighting the enemy, that it was for the greater good of the nation and that it came with the territory of the job.

The other girls saw me role-playing and thought I'd lost my mind. Angel just winked at me. I knew she was role-playing her own version of my fantasy. Little did the other girls know what we'd created. We thought that they were the ones who had lost their minds for not finding a bit of make-believe to get them through each day.

I was enjoying my fantasy and had gone so far as to invent a special set of spy equipment for myself, such as a lipstick poison dart and a compact mirror semaphore signaller, when suddenly one day I got a really bad stomach pain. Spy or not, I was laid very low.

I was unable to move, unable to do the job and unable to respond even when the madam was yelling at me and hitting me with any object within her reach. In my delirium, I reached for my lipstick poison dart and tried to fire it at her.

My illness was not unusual. The madam had to deal with at least two of us girls being out of action at any one time. This was simply bad for business, and the madam had to act to protect her income, or she, in turn, would be punished by those up a level from her on the poisoned pyramid. Her aim would be to get me back on my feet so that I could be back on my back in the fastest time possible and for the lowest cost. If she could have jolted me back to work with a loose electric wire, she would have done just that.

I lost consciousness and woke up a day later with a strange man looking down at me. It was a Nigerian man who said he was a nurse. He told me that I had an infection of the pelvis. It was a pelvic inflammatory disease due to either chlamydia or gonorrhoea – a sexually transmitted infection, anyway. The madam was standing over his shoulder as he turned around, and he gave her a collection of pills. I was told by the madam that I was to take these over the next few days.

Angel told me later, when we were supposed to be sleeping, that she, too, had suffered this pain before. It was an infection from one of the men, and it would go away if I took the pills. Angel told me that if I didn't, the rumour was that I'd never be able to have a child. I thought, *who would want to bring a child into a world like this, anyway? Why should I take the pills? Perhaps the infection might even kill me. Perhaps that would be a good way to die.* Angel persuaded me to take the pills so as to survive as a secret agent, not because the madam wanted me to. It was thrilling having Angel talk to me in a whisper as a fellow secret agent. I hadn't enjoyed anything as much as this.

Life went back to normal or what was at least near normal for me. I continued to indulge in make-believe stories with Angel while we actively continued our research. We had begun to think of how to contact the police and other relevant authorities when it all came crashing down. It began with a fever that wouldn't go away, and just like that, my house of cards came crashing down.

9

HUMANITARIAN SYSTEM

I lie now in this hospital room with my terminal diagnosis of stage 4 HIV. The doctors have gently explained that there is not much they can do at this stage except keep me as comfortable as possible. It is far too late, the disease has advanced too much and the fighters of my body's immune system have given up. I smiled sardonically when they told me the news. Who could blame my immune system for wanting out after the hell we have been through?

Ironically, my hospital room has turned out to be the best accommodation I have ever called mine. I guess life sometimes pokes fun that way.

I find myself going through all the research I have done, the work I began before my illness and have continued in this hospital room. I knew when I received my diagnosis that I had to finish my research, to get this story out there. It has become my purpose, my mission.

I will now share with you everything that I have learnt so that by the time you are done reading this, you will have a clearer understanding of how dire the situation of human trafficking is.

Let's start from the very beginning, shall we? Let's start where it began, in the country I call home, Nigeria.

You see, when a situation goes wrong, there is more than just one cause. In Nigeria, the National Agency for Prohibition of Trafficking in Persons (NAPTIP) was established in 2003 to provide trafficked people with a second chance.

The agency aims to provide support to victims of trafficking through monetary compensation, ensuring their social rehabilitation. The agency also provides a transient rehabilitation centre, which is supposed to offer safety to the victims of trafficking. This service lasts for a maximum period of six weeks. However, what measures are actually put in place to prevent trafficking, and how effective are these measures? How 'safe' are these shelters? How much protection is really available for those who have come from such a horrific experience?

The answers to these questions are difficult to provide. When I was at Madam's house, there was an unspoken rule among us girls to never talk about how we had got to where we were. However, I recall that one night, after one of the girls, Kamara, had come back to the house drunk after being with a customer, she had begun to talk to no one in particular about her previous life. She told us how a police officer had actually stopped the bus that had been smuggling her and some other girls, but he had allowed them to go without any questioning when a few naira notes were slipped into his hands. That was the first failure in the system, the first breach.

The one person who could have helped the situation and saved those girls failed to do so. I wonder how much money it took for him to turn a blind eye: two thousand naira? At any rate, it can't have been much.

The shelters that take in the rescued girls also share some blame for failing to fix the problem of human trafficking. The shelters do little to relieve the girls' trauma, and I have heard many stories about the poor conditions in these detention centres, including inadequate food and a lack of toiletries and proper medical care. Some girls complained about their inability to have visitors or contact their families, and some were kept from having proper communication with the NAPTIP officials. I shared some of the stories with Angel. She looked terrified and taken aback, but then she regained her composure. Anything is better than here, Samanta, she had said to me. I nodded back at her, though my feeling of unease remained. Were we going to escape our house of horrors just to land in another prison?

Well, I guess I will never personally find out, but for the sake of the other girls, I beseech you, dear reader, to look more into the horrors of human trafficking, as you are in a position to evoke change. Fight for our injustice as we are not able to.

Another important institution is the National Human

Rights Commission (NHRC), which was established by the National Human Rights Act of 1995. NHRC is saddled with promoting and protecting human rights in Nigeria. Other duties of this commission include investigating and monitoring all cases of human rights violations, fostering public enlightenment and education, facilitating conflict resolution, and providing assistance to the victims of abuse and other human rights violations. I wonder: would it have made a difference, perhaps, if I had been able to reach out to such an organisation?

Well, I guess I will never find out. I do hope, though, that other girls in my shoes will be able to make contact, and when they do, I really hope they will get a favourable and effective response. From what I know of the system in my country, their cries for help may fall on deaf ears. I can choose how hopeful I want to be about this situation. After all, everything else has already been decided.

I knew a lot about the NHRC from my research, but I hadn't really thought about it until one of the nurses I had entrusted with my story, Nurse Jackie, reminded me about the organisation. I told her my story because she had been particularly kind to me since my admission. Kindness is something I have experienced so little of in my short time on earth, so I soaked up all that she poured on me. I looked forward to the days she was on duty. She was appalled when I told her my story and seemed slightly in shock. She came into my hospital room early the next day, raving about how we needed to do something, inform the NHRC, etc. She understood the nature of my diagnosis, of course. She knew my time was nearly over; however, she wanted the people involved to be brought to justice. I smiled at her, buoyed by her exuberance. I assured her that there was nothing I wanted more than for these people to be brought to justice and for there to never be another Samanta, but this was a big ask, and it certainly went beyond the NHRC. I asked her if she had heard about the International Organization for Migration (IOM) before, but she replied in the negative. I took the opportunity to tell her about it.

The IOM is the principal intergovernmental body working in the field of migration. It encourages the entire international community to get involved in the fight against trafficking. The organisation is tasked with ensuring that migration occurs without the abuse of migrants' rights, and it assists migrants when they are in need. The other girls and I had so many options; we had so many people we could have reached out to, but with no means of reaching them, our attempts would have been futile. The traffickers kept us locked in a cage of our own fear, ignorance and superstition, a cage that prevented us from daring to make a move even when we began to see that we had options. For that crime alone, the perpetrators deserve the hottest places in hell.

Finally, the United Nations Children's Fund (UNICEF) is one of the most recognisable social welfare organisations as it is present in 192 countries and territories. It is concerned with immunisation, education, nutrition, improving sanitation for children and providing emergency relief, among numerous other functions. It is at the forefront of the fight for children's welfare and a better life for all children. I believe that UNICEF has a role to play in this delicate issue.

I will stop here for now. Please forgive whatever gaps exist in the information I have provided as I am only grasping at whatever I can find. But through all of my research, one thing has been made clear: there are a lot of well-meaning organisations that exist; however, trafficking remains at an all-time high. There are huge gaps in these systems, mainly regarding funding and execution. It is also necessary to implement organisations at local levels that will also be tasked with ensuring the welfare of young ladies and confronting sex trafficking rings.

Let's try to lend our voices to this struggle. This is my fervent plea to you, and know that despite what I have been through, the world is not all bad. I know that there are a lot of well-meaning, kind-hearted people out there that are unaware of the extent of the evil that goes on and what can be done about it, just like Nurse Jackie. As humans, we sometimes unintentionally overlook that which does not directly concern us. All I ask is that you remember that anyone could be a Samanta, so please consider lending your help to this cause. If this book reaches you and you are involved in the organisations I mentioned above, then I hope it becomes the catalyst that prompts you to look closer at the day-to-day running of your organisations and how effective your policies really are.

At this point, you might be wondering what the Italian government has to say about all these heinous crimes that take place on its shores. Well, the government places the responsibility on victims of trafficking to come forward and file a complaint. If a complaint is made, there is a system through which the Italian police can alert the Nigerian authorities to provide protection to the victim's family members in Nigeria. But if you have read until this point, you will understand by now the nature of the Nigerian law enforcement agencies. It is clear that their efforts are largely ineffective.

Hence, girls like me stay silent; we take the abuse and the pain and accept malnourishment to protect ourselves and our families. Some girls make it out eventually, the lucky ones, while the unlucky ones, like me, end up on a hospital bed or worse.

Since being diagnosed with HIV/AIDS, I have had one piece of luck. Just one. It was the great fortune of being able to educate myself a little more about the humanitarian system that exists globally and how it is working and failing. I am a victim of its failures, but I refuse to let that be my epitaph. I have educated myself to put my personal story, the one I share with thousands, into context and see some good come from the undeniably bad things that have happened to me. I am not a human rights lawyer – certainly not. Though I now like to imagine, as I once did in the past, that I became a spy. With time on my side, I might have studied, taken a law degree and specialised in this field. It is my specialist subject, after all.

10

THE LUCKY, THE UNLUCKY, AND THE LOST

Those who survive take one of two routes: they finally pay off their debt and are able to move on and attempt to pick up the pieces of their lives, or they continue down the path of pain and suffering, either as prostitutes for life until their bodies are no longer acceptable to men or until they themselves become madams.

They are known as the lucky and the unlucky, respectively.

Then there is a third group. They are the ones who don't make it. They die en route or on the job, or they take their own lives. Some even go missing, whether during the journey or at the destination in Europe. They are all known as the lost.

For the lucky who pay their debts and move on, the road is arduous. I saw only a minority of girls achieve this route. They are few and far between. They must be wily and navigate the internal politics of convincing their debtors to allow them to leave even when the debt is paid.

The debtors do not wish to say yes for a variety of reasons. Knowing what you know now about my story, I'm sure that doesn't surprise you. They fear being exposed to local European authorities and the risk of imprisonment or deportation. They fear competition if the lucky escapee wishes to start her own business, thus affecting their financial well-being. Lastly, they fear 'the lucky' returning home to Nigeria, where they could warn future girls and their families of the lies and deceit that potentially await them. Madam Gift certainly wouldn't want that, and she's higher up in the pyramid, so the debtor will absolutely not wish for that to happen.

If wishes were fishes. I was born into a land of voodoo and superstition. There is an old Nigerian proverb that says, 'Not to know is bad; not to want to know is worse.' In the case of us lucky, unlucky and lost... I'm not so sure.

For the unlucky who remain in the job for prolonged periods of time, they may never be able to achieve a semblance of the normalcy they were promised at the beginning. The physical wear and tear of the job, the psychological trauma of the constant punishment and false promises and the emotional turmoil of lost relationships and broken hope result in expedited ageing and frailty.

In my case, my dream of and journey to Europe led to one of the worst outcomes possible. A slow, painful death. I honestly would not have wanted to know how bad this would be and am glad that I didn't at the time of my diagnosis.

I saw many girls become women and women become old women without moving on from the job. They possess no other skills and need the job to survive and pay for their daily needs. One by one, as they age, their client numbers drop off, until these women can no longer sustain their livelihood. At that point, the madam discards them to the street, as they can no longer afford the rent and provide no monetary benefit.

I hear stories of these unlucky wandering the streets, turning to alcohol, drugs or petty crime until, oftentimes, they suffer an untimely death.

My friend Angel, the hand-holding whisperer and fellow imaginary spy, went down this route. I like to think that she is out there begging but still imagining that she's the new female James Bond.

Yet another group of the unlucky see an opportunity where others do not. They embrace the position and the role. I barely want to admit it, and I cannot understand it, but it seems that some of them enjoy the job. These women rise up the ranks, playing politics with the madam and one another, until one day they take the mantle. They are the new madams, taking advantage of their increased earnings and position to continue the process. To me, they are the unlucky because they cannot see the error of their ways.

Madam Gift is the unluckiest of them all in this story. She may feel lucky, but her day of reckoning will come.

For the lost, I feel envy. I wish I'd had the good luck or

the courage to be one myself. I saw and heard of many girls dying on the journey due to illness, drowning, exhaustion, accident or violence. In my view, they won the lottery, for they never knew what was coming. They died believing they were making a good decision.

Then there were some who ran away. They saved up enough money to buy a train ticket out of town and had enough courage to go through with it in spite of the utter fear of getting caught. A few didn't even have enough money. They resorted to begging at the train stations to be able to afford a journey out of town and far away from their captors.

Yet others died on the job, beaten by men, infected by men, overtaken by physical stress and even taking their own lives. I was never blessed by instant death at the hands of another. I wish I had been. I also did not have the courage to do it myself. I have not seen or heard from my family in years, but I always knew that without my earnings, they would suffer. For them, I could not become lost.

11

THE CYCLE

There is a vicious cycle at work here. This makes everything being done by the politicians and third-sector organisations seem futile at times.

The priests in Nigeria make money by putting curses on women who are forced into trafficking by the juju man and his hurricane lamp circle of pain.

Women in Nigeria working in trade and commerce once travelled to Italy to buy the leatherwork, lace materials and fabric and came home to sell it, but the economy collapsed in 1980. So the commerce dried up, and the women stayed in Italy working on farms. But then the work on farms in Italy started to decline as well, so they had to resort to prostitution. Then these women started to realise how lucrative prostitution is. They started recruiting from their families in Nigeria, and the first generation of victims became madams... thus, the cycle started.

They came home and showed off their wealth and their kangaroo-shaped handbags and appeared to be doing well financially. The families that saw them wanted their children to be like that. It was a way out of poverty, and who wouldn't want that?

The girls who are forced into prostitution today are getting progressively younger. The debt requires girls to make more money. This means that to pay off their debts, they become in charge of other girls, leading them into the madam role.

The debts signed up to are vague and confusing. Think about what happened to me. Most women think they are going to Europe to earn money. Once they realise their situation, it is very scary for them. They slowly but surely understand that there is no way out for them but prostitution. Thus, the cycle perpetuates.

There are systemic factors that make the cycle hard to stop: poverty, social stigma and family rejection for the girls if they can return, immigration policies, bribes... to name but a few.

Mentally, it is so hard to break the cycle after being physically and emotionally abused and left with no money. Remember me, sobbing on that floor and then the small comfort of holding Angel's hand.

Italy has been the stage for a cruel cycle of exploitation in which survivors of trafficking, after years of forced prostitution, have become traffickers themselves, the so-called 'madams'. Some of them bring new women to Italy in order to finish paying off their debt to their traffickers and find a way out of the streets, and others have been exploited for so long that they see exploitation of others as their only option for a better life.[1]

In Libya, where I spent an unpleasant week or two, there are the jailers, the individuals who profit from being the middlemen. They aren't going to want to give up their slice of the pie any time soon.

If anti-immigrant sentiment continues in Europe and visas are denied, women forced into sex trafficking will be less likely to come forward and will have fewer protections, and the ones in charge of the organisations will continue to profit as women suffer. Remember Madam Gift's eight-thousand-dollar car?

Since the 2018 Salvini Decree, it has become harder for victims to renew their immigration status. Conflict within Nigeria has led to displacement, and that exacerbates women's and girls' vulnerability to trafficking. Nigeria has escalating child protection problems, with a large number of children out of school and increased violence against children.

Then there is poverty and inequality. According to the World Bank, more than half of all Nigerians live in absolute poverty, with women making up a large portion of this

---

1   https://www.theguardian.com/world/2020/aug/27/nigeria-italy-human-trafficking-sex-workers-exploitation-justice

group. This causes real and present gender inequality for women in Nigeria.

Now we come to the C-word: corruption.

Nigeria ranked 144th out of 180 countries in the 2018 Corruption Perceptions Index by Transparency International. According to a 2017 report by the United Nations Office on Drugs and Crime, 'The vast majority of bribery episodes in Nigeria are initiated either directly or indirectly by public officials and almost 70 per cent of bribes are paid before a service is rendered.'

Law enforcement and the judiciary are areas of particular concern according to the study, which also says that roughly 400 billion Nigerian naira (approximately $1.1 billion) is spent on bribes each year and that Nigerians consider bribery the third most important problem facing their country.

I think I know what the first problem is.

12

LET'S TALK

L et's talk. Let's talk about being proactive, not reactive. Let's not forget prevention. Primary prevention here will stand for the government making such journeys as mine unattractive. Secondary prevention will be stopping these girls from leaving the shores of their country illegally.

The role of parents will be to recognise traffickers and offers of jobs to their children that sound suspicious. Also, female children displaying wealth that is unaccounted for is to be treated as suspicious rather than being blindly celebrated. Parents must be ready to strive for their child's well-being and, when unable to do so, must call for help. It is injustice, a crime, for parents to know that their child is going to be trafficked into any type of slavery and for them to support it for their own material gain.

If you are a leader in society, in any capacity, I believe you have a role in educating as well as putting measures in place to make the exploitation of young girls difficult. Country, state and regional leaders should ensure education is affordable or, better still, free for all children, especially girls. African leaders must work really hard to reduce inequality between the rich and the poor and make essential public amenities easy to afford, including food, education and health. The brain drain will not end in underdeveloped countries unless they develop. Can I add that the developed countries have a role in ensuring that underdeveloped countries develop? If developed countries continue to accept our experts and professionals, they must also be ready to accept our law offenders and criminals. Creating jobs that are adequate to take care of essential needs will reduce illegal migration by over 50per cent. This is the first step in the right direction, and the citizens of this country must begin to clamour for their fundamental human rights.

The madams must see the girls they exploit first as human beings and then as their daughters. They should imagine someone else inflicting a lifetime of pain on them or their daughters. Individuals who know these madams must report them to law enforcement agents or speak up. They must refuse to collect their ill-gotten wealth in exchange for silence. Investigations should be opened up by the law enforcement agents to target madams and stop them before more girls are deceived. Returned girls should be reintegrated into society and should not be worshipped for their wealth.

A number of governmental and non-governmental organisations are doing a lot. Billions of dollars are being spent to combat this ugly trend, but the reality is that success will be achieved only with a multifaceted approach. I suggest a triangular approach in which these international organisations are at the centre of a strong action- and information-sharing network, with the governments of involved countries, the International Police (Interpol) and local agencies being the three points. In turn, local agencies should get information from citizens and act on it. Women like me also have human rights, and just because I can't fight for myself, it does not mean I should suffer. Humanitarian organisations have to stand up to the challenges of fighting for these girls and women. Advocacy to strengthen human rights laws against prostitution must never stop, and international organisations must budget a good amount of funding for advocacy. Lastly, if UN women can hear me, can I ask you to take a lead in this serious matter, as these girls look up to you for help?

Your role as an individual ranges from reporting suspicious activities to standing up against injustice and human rights abuses against women and girls. We need more activists to say that enough is enough. We need people to go all out, in spite of the inconvenience, to fight for girls that have been put into everlasting bondage. I want people who can leave their comfort zone and make a plan to stop a new Samanta Orobosa Matama from being exploited and molested. Do you want to know how many new Samantas are deceived every day? They are in their hundreds. You can start by wearing t-shirts and making t-shirts that read 'NO TO SEX SLAVERY' and that will be sent to endemic zones. Humanitarian organisations are overwhelmed with increasing humanitarian problems worldwide and are counting on you to fill the gap. There are limited resources, too, so these organisations count on your donations as well. Would you stand by today and let another Samanta die?

If you work for an agency, group or team that facilitates female immigration for the purpose of prostitution, then this is for you. You have successfully ruined my life, and now my time is up. Congratulations. What you do not know is that, despite all your ill-gotten wealth, connections and power, your time will soon be up. Evil cannot win forever. Thus, my advice to you is to stop aiding prostitution and start using your resources to aid development. You can always be forgiven for the pain you have caused millions of girls out there but only if you have a change of mind and start investing in these girls. Well, I don't have much more to say to you people. A word is enough for the wise.

To the law enforcement agents, the world knows what you have been doing. You have been letting us down when we needed you most. You have been collecting bribes and turning blind eyes when you could have been saving us from a life of pain and suffering. Can I appeal to your conscience to do the jobs of protection and prosecution, the ones you pledged to do when you took the law enforcement oath, and not the job of crime and destruction? You are our last hope. We saw you in the past as our heroes. Why don't you go back to that place? Please stop receiving bribes from traffickers, stop listening to instructions from politicians and start advising your government on the things to do to end the menace of sex trafficking.

I feel my life ebbing from me. I can barely hold my pen. Maybe I need to go and rest... but before then, I have one thing to say to everyone. I say, together we stand, divided we fall. This is...

EPILOGUE

I am Jackie Francesca Giovanni of the San Roco Hospital, Rome. I provided palliative care to Samanta Orobosa Matama, and when we pronounced her dead, I carefully removed this long letter from her hands. I will see that her story is published for all the world to know that there once lived a woman called Samanta Orobosa Matama.

REFERENCES

Thank you to the following websites for providing us with information for the later chapters.

- www.hrw.org

- www.theguardian.com

- etd.uwc.ac.za

- www.upr-info.org

ABOUT THE AUTHOR

 Dr Olalekan Ogungbemi is a distinguished physician and humanitarian. Based in Scotland, the graduate of the prestigious Igbinedion University has long left his prints on the sands of caring for vulnerable people in society through the activities of his non-governmental organisation, the Moole Charity Foundation. The foundation provides free and inclusive medical check-up, provision of scholarships, hospital and prison outreaches. Dr Ogungbemi's work with people who are internally displaced and victims of human trafficking in his home country Nigeria instigated his desire to write this book. He is an award-winning doctor with a master's degrees in Public Health and Humanitarian Health from the University of South Wales and John Hopkins University.

ABOUT THE CO-AUTHORS

Dr Ali Karim is first and foremost a selfless individual who has a passion for helping the less privileged through his non-governmental organisation, Global Shout. An internal medicine physician trained at the prestigious Georgetown University, he is the son of Afghan refugees who immigrated to the United States following the USSR invasion of Afghanistan in 1979. Through his organisation, he has provided avenues to gaining secondary education, access to water wells and has built hospitals to in countries such as Afghanistan, Nepal and Ecuador. His humanitarian services extend to the unification of Korean families as well as providing medical and translation services while working with United Airline. Outside of his medical commitments, Dr Ali has made a name as an international documentary filmmaker.

Hannah Kirsch is a humanitarian par excellence. A graduate of Brandeis University with a master's in Social Work from the University of California, she has dedicated her time to the public child welfare system. She works with children who have been abused and or sex-trafficked as part of her duties as a Clinical Social Worker in Los Angeles. She is currently pursuing a master's in Applied Science in Humanitarian Health at Johns Hopkins University.